Piano · Vocal · Guitar

Best of
KENNY CHESNEY

Cover Photo by Allister Ann

ISBN 978-1-5400-2604-0

Visit Hal Leonard Online at
www.halleonard.com

Contact Us:
Hal Leonard
7777 West Bluemound Road
Milwaukee, WI 53213
Email: info@halleonard.com

In Europe contact:
Hal Leonard Europe Limited
Distribution Centre, Newmarket Road
Bury St Edmunds, Suffolk, IP33 3YB
Email: info@halleonardeurope.com

In Australia contact:
Hal Leonard Australia Pty. Ltd.
4 Lentara Court
Cheltenham, Victoria, 3192 Australia
Email: info@halleonard.com.au

Contents

ALL THE PRETTY GIRLS

Words and Music by TOMMY LEE JAMES,
JOSH OSBORNE and NICOLLE GALYON

*Recorded a half step lower.

AMERICAN KIDS

Words and Music by LUKE LAIRD,
SHANE McANALLY and RODNEY DALE CLAWSON

BEER IN MEXICO

Words and Music by
KENNY CHESNEY

Moderately fast

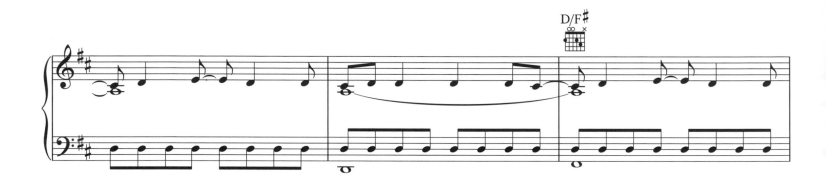

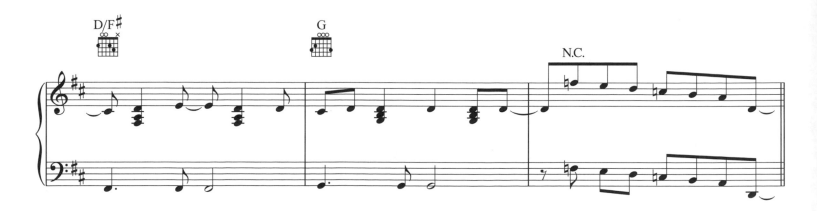

May - be I'll   set - tle down,

20

COME OVER

Words and Music by SHANE McANALLY,
JOSH OSBORNE and SAM HUNT

*Recorded a half step lower.

For - get _

a-bout your friends, you know _ they're gon-na say we're bad _ for each oth-er, but we _ ain't good for an-y-one else. _

D.S. al Coda

CODA

We don't have to miss _ each oth - er. _ Come o - ver. _

THE BOYS OF FALL

Words and Music by CASEY BEATHARD
and DAVE TURNBULL

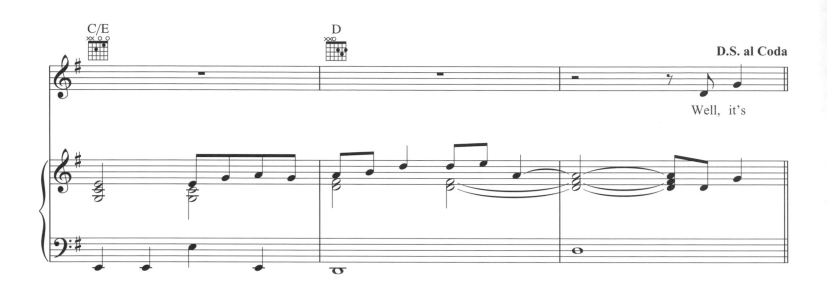

D.S. al Coda

Well, it's

the boys ___ of fall. ___

DON'T BLINK

Words and Music by CASEY BEATHARD
and CHRIS WALLIN

SHE THINKS MY TRACTOR'S SEXY

Words and Music by JIM COLLINS
and PUAL OVERSTREET

N.C.

Repeat and Fade

Optional Ending

THE GOOD STUFF

Words and Music by CRAIG WISEMAN
and JIM COLLINS

HOW FOREVER FEELS

Words and Music by WENDELL MOBLEY
and TONY MULLINS

NO SHOES NO SHIRT
(No Problems)

Words and Music by
CASEY BEATHARD

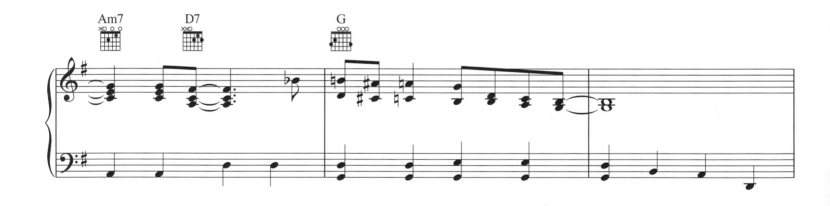

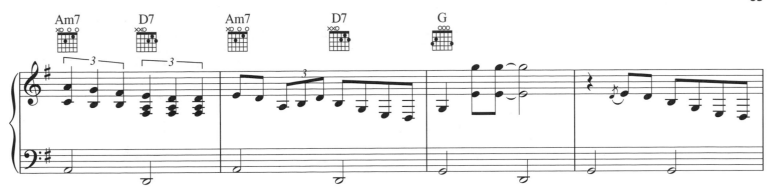

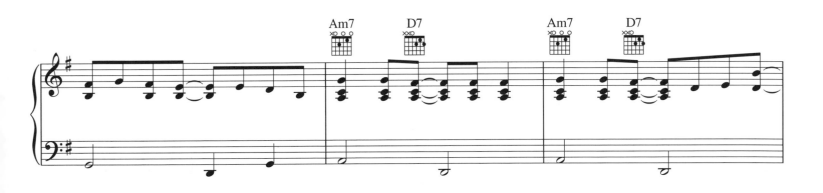

I've been up _____ to my neck work-in' six _____
_____ on a chair _ and the sand _

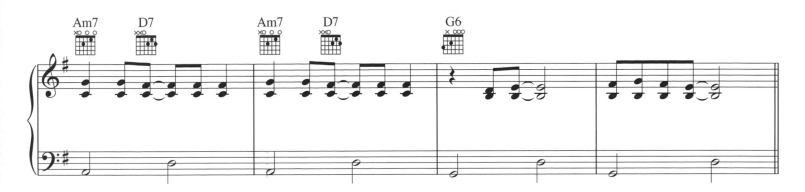

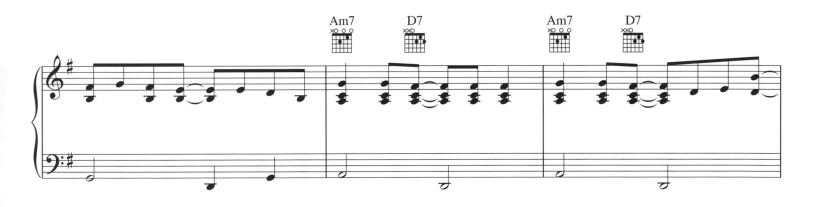

PIRATE FLAG

Words and Music by ROSS COPPERMAN
and DAVID LEE MURPHY

71

D

back in the woods, __ yeah, __ life was good. __

C

But here we are in a

D

D.S. al Coda

lo - cal bar, ___ drink - in' shoot - in' stars. __

I might spend my

CODA

D

pi - rate flag __ and an is - land girl. __

Am

G

A pi - rate flag __ and an is - land girl. __

D

SAVE IT FOR A RAINY DAY

Words and Music by ANDREW DORFF,
BRAD TURSI and MATT RAMSEY

Slow Country groove

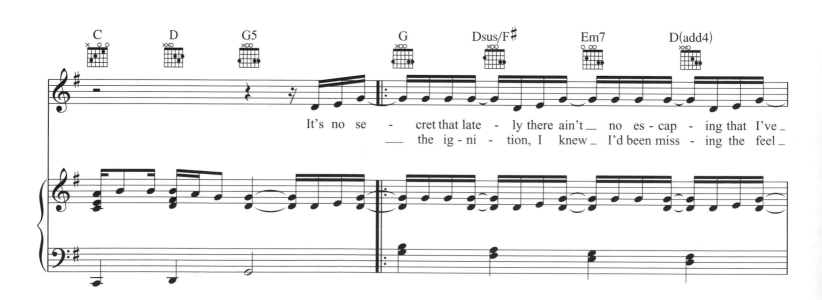

It's no se - cret that late - ly there ain't __ no es - cap - ing that I've __

__ the ig - ni - tion, I knew __ I'd been miss - ing the feel __

too cold to be think-in' 'bout you. Gon-na take ___ this heart-break and tuck it a - way, ___ save ___

___ it for a rain - y day. ___

When I turned ___ it for a rain - y day. ___ Yeah, the mu-

- sic's too good, and my friends ___ are all out, and they're all ___ too high to be bring-in' 'em down. ___ If they ask ___

SETTING THE WORLD ON FIRE

Words and Music by ROSS COPPERMAN,
JOSH OSBORNE and MATT JENKINS

Male: Yeah, we got drunk on La Ci - e - ne - ga Bou - le - vard, tak - in' pic - tures of peo - ple we thought were stars. It's eas - y to give in to your heart

SOMEWHERE WITH YOU

Words and Music by SHANE McANALLY
and JOHN THOMAS HARDING

If you're go - in' out

SUMMERTIME

Words and Music by STEVE McEWAN
and CRAIG WISEMAN

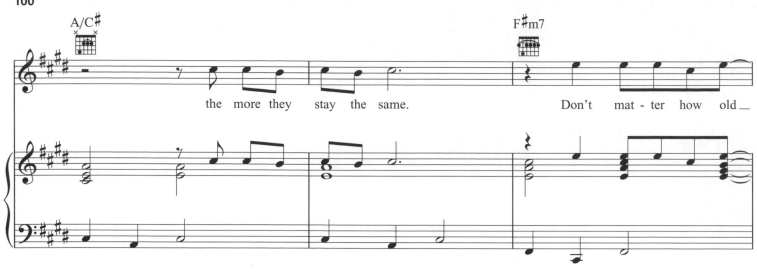

the more they stay the same. Don't mat-ter how old__

D.S. al Coda

__ you are, __ when you know __ what I'm talk - in' 'bout. Yeah, ba - by, when you got

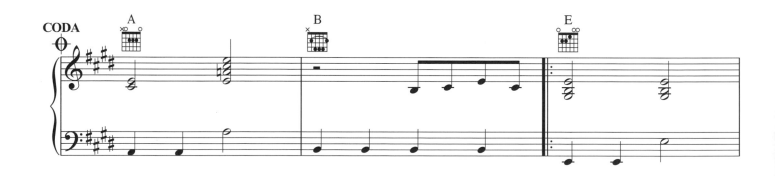

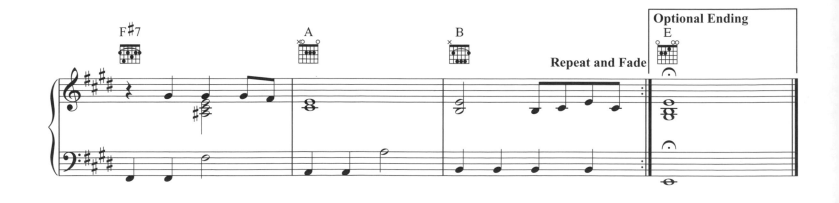

WHO YOU'D BE TODAY

Words and Music by AIMEE MAYO
and BILL LUTHER

Moderately fast

Sun - ny days seem to hurt the most. ___ I wear the pain like a
see the world, would you chase your dreams? ___ Set - tle down with a

heav - y coat. ___ I feel you ev - 'ry - where ___ I go. ___
fam - i - ly? ___ I won - der what would you name your ba -

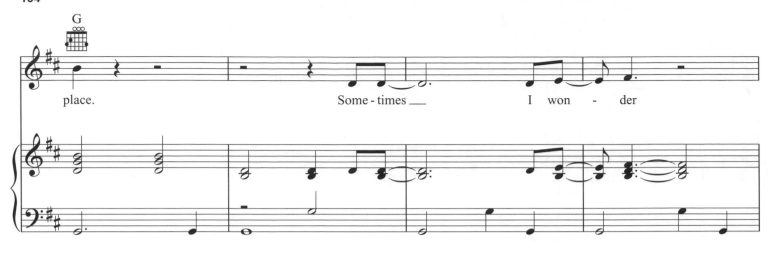

place.   Some - times ___   I won - der

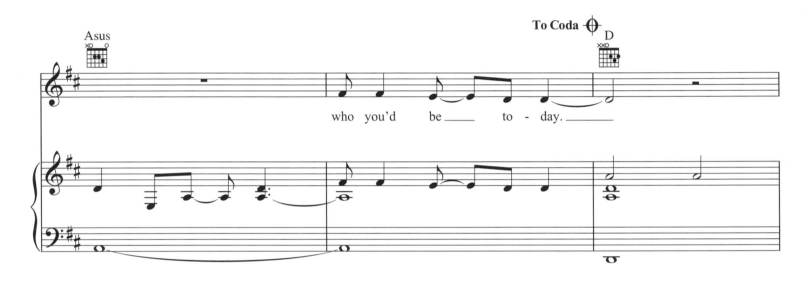

who you'd   be ___   to - day. ___

D.S. al Coda

Would you

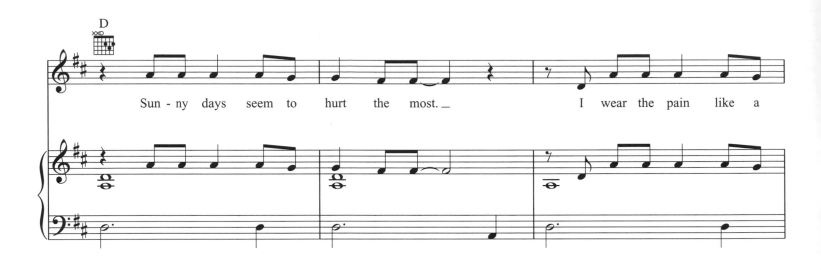

Sun - ny days seem to hurt the most. __ I wear the pain like a

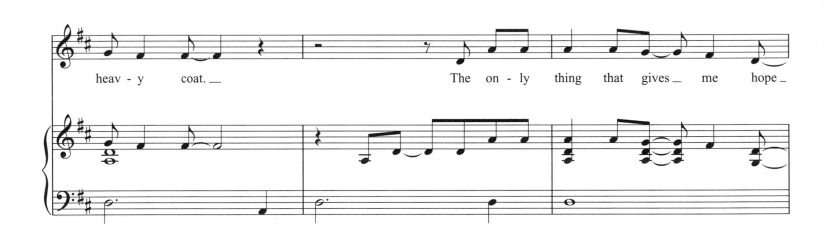

heav - y coat. __ The on - ly thing that gives __ me hope __

is I know __ I'll

THERE GOES MY LIFE

Words and Music by NEIL THRASHER
and WENDELL MOBLEY

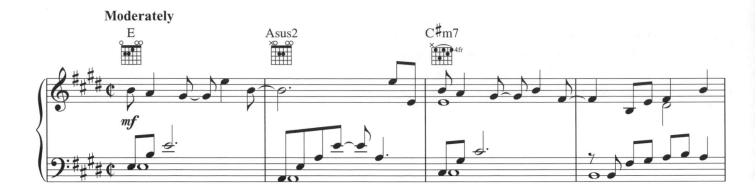

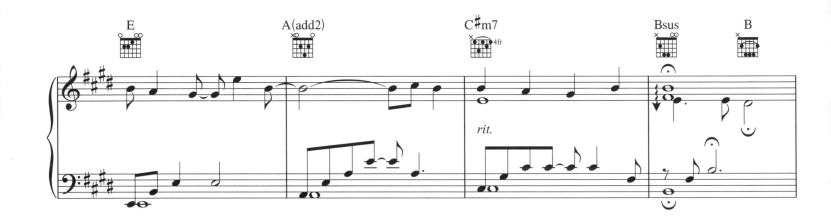

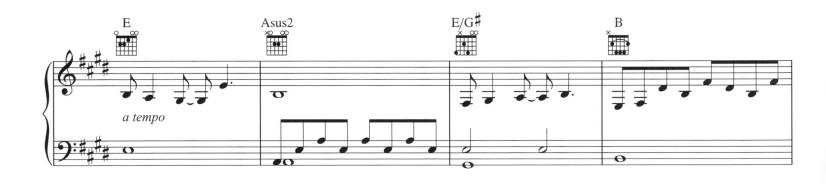

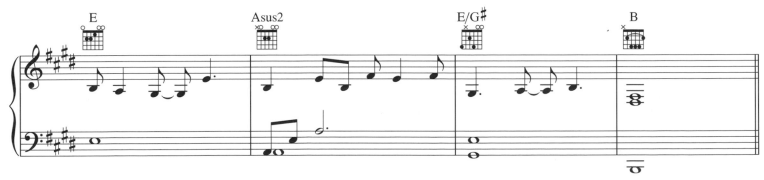

114

115

WHEN THE SUN GOES DOWN

Words and Music by
BRETT JAMES

118

sun goes_ down._

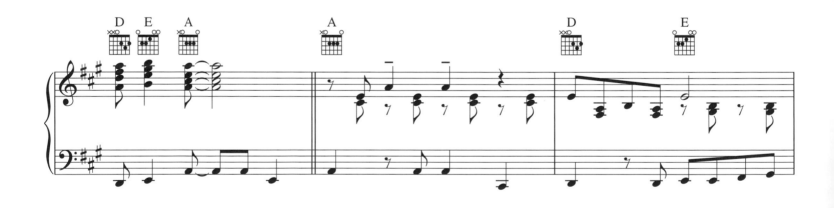

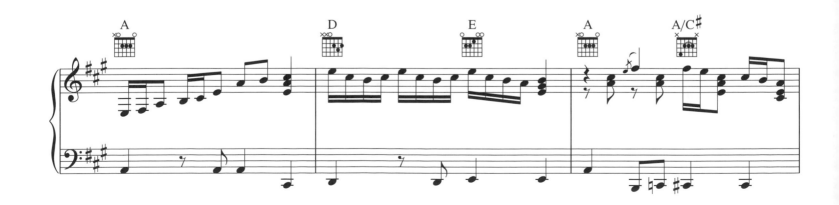

YOU AND TEQUILA

Words and Music by MATRACA BERG
and DEANA CARTER

* *Recorded a half step lower.*

nev - er ___ e - nough. ___ When it comes ___

___ to you, oh, the dam - age I ___ could do.

It's al - ways your fav - 'rite sins ___ that do ___

YOU HAD ME FROM HELLO

Words and Music by SKIP EWING
and KENNY CHESNEY

133

HAL LEONARD COUNTRY DECADE SERIES

THE 1950s

50 country golden oldies, including: Ballad of a Teenage Queen • Cold, Cold Heart • El Paso • Heartaches by the Number • Heartbreak Hotel • Hey, Good Lookin' • I Walk the Line • In the Jailhouse Now • Jambalaya (On the Bayou) • Sixteen Tons • Tennessee Waltz • Walkin' After Midnight • Your Cheatin' Heart • and more.
00311283 Piano/Vocal/Guitar $15.99

THE 1970s

41 songs, including: All the Gold in California • Coal Miner's Daughter • Country Bumpkin • The Devil Went to Georgia • The Gambler • Another Somebody Done Somebody Wrong Song • If We Make It Through December • Lucille • Sleeping Single in a Double Bed • and more.
00311285 Piano/Vocal/Guitar $15.99

THE 1980s

40 country standards, including: All My Ex's Live in Texas • The Chair • Could I Have This Dance • Coward of the County • Drivin' My Life Away • Elvira • Forever and Ever, Amen • God Bless the U.S.A. • He Stopped Loving Her Today • I Was Country When Country Wasn't Cool • Islands in the Stream • On the Road Again • Tennessee Flat Top Box • To All the Girls I've Loved Before • and more.
00311282 Piano/Vocal/Guitar $15.99

THE 1990s

40 songs, including: Achy Breaky Heart (Don't Tell My Heart) • Amazed • Blue • Boot Scootin' Boogie • Down at the Twist and Shout • Friends in Low Places • Here's a Quarter (Call Someone Who Cares) • Man! I Feel like a Woman! • She Is His Only Need • Wide Open Spaces • You Had Me from Hello • You're Still the One • and more.
00311280 Piano/Vocal/Guitar $16.95

THE 2000s – 2nd Edition

35 contemporary country classics, including: Alcohol • American Soldier • Beer for My Horses • Blessed • Breathe • Have You Forgotten? • I Am a Man of Constant Sorrow • I Hope You Dance • I'm Gonna Miss Her (The Fishin' Song) • Long Black Train • No Shoes No Shirt (No Problems) • Redneck Woman • and more.
00311281 Piano/Vocal/Guitar $16.99

THE 2010s – 2nd Edition

35 modern hits: All About Tonight • Better Dig Two • Cruise • Die a Happy Man • Girl Crush • The House That Built Me • Just a Kiss • Mean • Pontoon • Something in the Water • Stay • Take Your Time • Tennessee Whiskey • Wanted • You Should Be Here • and more.
00175237 Piano/Vocal/Guitar $17.99

HAL•LEONARD®

Visit Hal Leonard online at
www.halleonard.com

THE BEST EVER
COLLECTION
ARRANGED FOR PIANO, VOICE AND GUITAR

100 of the Most Beautiful Piano Solos Ever
100 songs
00102787 .... $27.50

150 of the Most Beautiful Songs Ever
150 ballads
00360735 .... $27.00

More of the Best Acoustic Rock Songs Ever
69 tunes
00311738 .... $19.95

Best Acoustic Rock Songs Ever
65 acoustic hits
00310984 .... $22.99

Best Big Band Songs Ever
68 big band hits
00359129 .... $17.99

Best Blues Songs Ever
73 blues tunes
00312874 .... $19.99

Best Broadway Songs Ever
83 songs
00309155 .... $24.99

More of the Best Broadway Songs Ever
82 songs
00311501 .... $22.95

Best Children's Songs Ever
101 songs
00159272 .... $19.99

Best Christmas Songs Ever
69 holiday favorites
00359130 .... $24.99

Best Classic Rock Songs Ever
64 hits
00310800 .... $22.99

Best Classical Music Ever
86 classical favorites
00310674 (Piano Solo) $19.95

The Best Country Rock Songs Ever
52 hits
00118881 .... $19.99

Best Country Songs Ever
78 classic country hits
00359135 .... $19.99

Best Disco Songs Ever
50 songs
00312565 .... $19.99

Best Dixieland Songs Ever
90 songs
00312326 .... $19.99

Best Early Rock 'n' Roll Songs Ever
74 songs
00310816 .... $19.95

Best Easy Listening Songs Ever
75 mellow favorites
00359193 .... $19.99

Best Folk/Pop Songs Ever
66 hits
00138299 .... $19.99

Best Gospel Songs Ever
80 gospel songs
00310503 .... $19.99

Best Hymns Ever
118 hymns
00310774 .... $18.99

Best Jazz Piano Solos Ever
80 songs
00312079 .... $19.99

Best Jazz Standards Ever
77 jazz hits
00311641 .... $19.95

More of the Best Jazz Standards Ever
74 beloved jazz hits
00311023 .... $19.95

Best Latin Songs Ever
67 songs
00310355 .... $19.99

Best Love Songs Ever
62 favorite love songs
00359198 .... $19.99

Best Movie Songs Ever
71 songs
00310063 .... $19.99

Best Movie Soundtrack Songs Ever
70 songs
00146161 .... $17.99

Best Pop/Rock Songs Ever
50 classics
00138279 .... $19.99

Best Praise & Worship Songs Ever
80 all-time favorites
00311057 .... $22.99

Best R&B Songs Ever
66 songs
00310184 .... $19.95

Best Rock Songs Ever
63 songs
00490424 .... $18.95

Best Showtunes Ever
71 songs
00118782 .... $19.99

Best Songs Ever
71 must-own classics
00265721 .... $24.99

Best Soul Songs Ever
70 hits
00311427 .... $19.95

Best Standards Ever, Vol. 1 (A-L)
72 beautiful ballads
00359231 .... $17.95

Best Standards Ever, Vol. 2 (M-Z)
73 songs
00359232 .... $17.99

Best Torch Songs Ever
70 sad and sultry favorites
00311027 .... $19.95

Best Wedding Songs Ever
70 songs
00311096 .... $19.95

0718